NICK GULLO'S
GUIDE

OPERATING A PROFESSIONAL
POKER ROOM

POKER RULES AND PROCEDURES

NICK GULLO

BONUS INCLUDED
TEXAS HOLD'EM STUDY GUIDE

authorHOUSE®

AuthorHouse™
1663 Liberty Drive
Bloomington, IN 47403
www.authorhouse.com
Phone: 1 (800) 839-8640

Published by AuthorHouse 11/22/2016

ISBN: 978-1-5246-4854-1 (sc)
ISBN: 978-1-5246-4853-4 (e)

Library of Congress Control Number: 2016918395

Print information available on the last page.

Any people depicted in stock imagery provided by Thinkstock are models, and such images are being used for illustrative purposes only. Certain stock imagery © Thinkstock.

This book is printed on acid-free paper.

For information and consulting contact:
Nick Gullo
Email: nickgullo@hotmail.com
Cell #: 702-788-8875

BONUS INCLUDED

TEXAS HOLD'EM
STUDY GUIDE
Beginning Players to Advanced Players

Contents

Poker Etiquette   Betting Terms

Cards Card Procedures Shuffle and Cut Procedures Dealing Procedures

Hand Rankings Wager Rules Rake Employee Rules Rack Chip Fills

Chip Runner Procedures   Brush Person Procedures

Big Blind Small Blind Button Procedures

Tournament Rules   Kill Pots   Bad Beat Jackpots   High Hand Jackpots

Game Procedures

Texas Hold'em   Seven Card Stud

Seven Card Stud Hi/Lo Split-Eight or Better

Omaha High Omaha Eight or Better

Pineapple Hold'em

Razz

Draw Poker Triple Draw Low Ball 2 to 7

Authored By: NICK GULLO

Supervisor of World Poker Tour Tournament
WSOP Satellite Supervisor
ISBN 0-9779301-0-6

Contents

About the Author

Nick Gullo is a native of New Orleans and a graduate of Southeastern Louisiana University. He also attended Loyola University Law School.

His father was a poker player and taught him the basics of the games and created a love of poker that has stayed with him throughout his life.

In 1965, Nick moved to Las Vegas to pursue a full time career in gaming.

Over the past 40 years, Nick has experienced almost every known position in the gaming industry. He started as a shill on Fremont St. and eventually became an owner of a small casino and the President of a Las Vegas Hotel/Casino.

He has written books and magazine articles on Casino Marketing and he taught at U.N.L.V. and Clark County Community College. He recently wrote a Texas Hold'em Study Guide for beginners to advanced players.

In 1998 he retired as the Vice President of Gaming of the Showboat Corp. to create and manage his own Gaming and Marketing Consulting firm and to devote more time to playing poker.

In 2000, Nick opened a poker room in Costa Rica and hosted some of the largest tournaments ever held in all of Central America.

In 2002, he brought the World Poker Tour to Costa Rica.

Acknowledgement

Thank you
Janine K. Gullo

This project would have been impossible without the encouragement and help from Janine.

She spent countless hours typing; editing and helping me research the material in this book.

Thank you
Jan Fisher

Her encouragement and contribution to this project was enormous, I especially thank her for allowing me to use her very extensive glossary.

Preface

The interest in poker has increased over the past three years at least tenfold.

This new found love for the game of poker, in all of it's various forms, has been created by several obvious factors:

1. The World Poker Tour
2. The World Series of Poker
3. Internet Gaming
4. Televising of Tournaments
5. Huge Tournament Prize Pools
6. Amateurs Winning Tournaments
7. Higher Participation of Female Players

When any sport or activity experiences this much new interest in such a short period of time, it creates a very large number of new and inexperienced players.

These novice players, like in any other sport, want to know as much about the rules and regulations of the game as possible.

It is even more so in poker because of the large number of games that are played at home, on the kitchen table, without the benefit of a professional dealer or supervisor.

Naturally, as situations arise that require higher level of technical expertise than is had by the home players, they need someone to be able to ask for a ruling, and if that "someone" is not available, they need a reference source.

When this happens, most of the players will ask, "How do they do it in Vegas"?

I am sure that almost every "well known" poker room in Nevada, California, Mississippi and other gaming jurisdictions has received a call late at night asking for a poker supervisor to answer a question for a player that is involved in a game at that moment.

I personally have received several of the above types of calls and have actually had a player ask me to put my answer in writing and fax it to him immediately so all the players in the game could read it.

I have been contacted by people, as individuals and as members of an organization that needed help with the rules and procedures to host an open game or a tournament.

A travel agent contacted me for advice on the rules for a tournament that he was putting on for a group of 85 people that he was bringing to a Caribbean resort. He had zero poker experience. He did not even know how to play Hold'em.

The purpose of this manual is to give some guidance to the players who need a ruling or at least an explanation of a rule that they can refer to as the need arises. It will also provide the needed procedures for running a game or a tournament.

This information contained herein was used in my poker rooms in Las Vegas, East Chicago, Indiana, and Costa Rica. Some poker rooms use a slight variation of these procedures but I am certain this manual will answer or at least address most of your questions. If you have any questions regarding this manual please feel free to contact me.

CHAPTER

1

POKER ETIQUETTE

Poker Etiquette

A player who expects to show down the winning hand should show it immediately; no slow rolls. If he has bet and been called, turn the cards up when the action is complete.

It is considered impolite to request to see the hand of a player who has just been beaten in a pot. This often may provoke or aggravate another player or players.

Although deception is a necessary part of poker, it is not polite to use an excessive amount of time to make a play one knows will be made.

Proper language and behavior should be a standard for poker players.

A player should not fold if there is no bet facing him, even in turn, if another player may gain an advantage over a competitor by the act.

A player going "all-in" should announce that fact.

A raise should be announced.

To assist the dealer in maintaining a comfortable fast pace of play, a player should turn all his cards facedown when folding.

If one expects to be leaving the game for a fairly long time, the supervisor should be notified. Players should know the rules in their respective cardrooms so they can pick up their chips if they will exceed the allotted time away from the game.

Lengthy discussions about a previous hand are unwelcome.

Criticism of the way another player has elected to play his hand, or his general style of play, is impolite and undesirable.

A player is entitled to quit the game any time he chooses without suffering criticism, unless a specified length of time is required and made known before play begins.

A player who shows his cards to another player at the conclusion of the hand must show it to the other players who request to see the hand. This is known as "show one, show all" and is a common rule in public cardrooms.

Players should assist the dealer by calling attention to an error in the amount of the bet or improper reading of a hand.

It is improper to make an effort to see another player's holecards by doing such things as leaning or ducking the head. It is proper for an opponent to complain when a player is constantly getting the opportunity to see another's holecards.

A player discarding his hand should release them on a low line of flight and at a moderate rate of speed. They should be directed only towards the muck, not the dealer's hands.

Talk or action demeaning to the dealer will not be tolerated. Throwing cards, name-calling and other such behavior will be grounds for suspending or barring any player from the cardroom.

A player should not read at the table if it interferes with or slows down the action. A cardroom may have a specific rule about reading at the table.

A player who folds may not make his cards known to the other players while the hand is in progress.

Players may not agree to "not bet" each other. This is a form of collusion.

A player cannot give an opinion about the contents of another player's hand while the hand is in progress.

A player may not receive help to play his hand. There can only be one player per hand.

CHAPTER

2

POKER HAND RANKINGS

Poker Hand Rankings

1. The rank of the cards used in poker for the determination of winning hands, in order of highest to lowest rank, shall be" ace, king, queen, jack, ten, nine, eight, seven, six, five, four, trey and deuce. For purposes of completing a "straight flush" or a "straight", an ace may be combined with a 2, 3, 4, and 5 or a ten, jack, queen, and king.

2. The high poker hands as determined by the holding of a full five-card hand, in order of highest to lowest rank:

   a. "Royal Flush", an ace, king, queen, jack, and ten of the same suit.

   b. "Straight Flush", five cards of the same suit in consecutive ranking, with king, queen, jack, ten, and nine being the highest ranking straight flush and ace, 2, 3, 4, and 5 being the lowest ranking straight flush.

   c. "Four-of-a-kind", four cards of the same rank, with four aces being the highest ranking four-of-a-kind and four deuces being the lowest ranking four-of-a-kind.

   d. "Full House", three-of-a-kind plus a pair with three aces full being the highest ranking full house and three deuces full being the lowest ranking full house.

   e. "Flush", five cards of the same suit with an ace, king, queen, jack, and ten being the highest ranking flush and an ace, 2, 3, 4, and 5 being lowest ranking flush.

   f. "Straight", five cards of consecutive rank, regardless of suit, with an ace, king, queen, jack, and ten being the highest ranking straight and an ace, 2, 3, 4, and 5 being the lowest ranking straight.

   g. "Three-of-a-kind", three cards of the same rank regardless of suit, with three aces being the highest-ranking three-of-a-kind and three deuces being the lowest ranking three-of-a-kind.

   h. "Two Pair", two pair with two aces and two kings being the highest ranking and two treys and two deuces being the lowest ranking two pair.

   i. "One Pair", two cards of the same rank, two aces being the highest and two deuces being the lowest.

   j. "High Card", a hand without a pair is determined by the highest-ranking cards. a hand containing an ace is the highest possible high card hand.

3. When comparing two hands that are of identical poker hand rank, the hand which contains the highest-ranking card as provided in one above or five below is considered the higher-ranking hand. If the hands are of identical rank after the application of this subsection, the hands are considered tied and the pot equally split among the players with the tied hands.

4. All suits are of equal value for determining the value of the poker hands at the showdown.

5. The rank of the cards used in low poker for the determination of winning hands is: ace, deuce, trey, four, five, six, seven, eight, nine, ten, jack, queen, and king.

6. For the purposes of determining a winning hand at low poker, straights and flushes do not exist, except in deuce to seven low.

7. The ranking of a low poker hand as determined by the holding of a full five-card hand is the opposite of the rankings for high poker as set forth in sections two and three above.

8. In all games of poker, a five-card hand is ranked according to the cards actually contained therein and not by the player's opinion or statement of its value; "Cards speak for themselves".

CHAPTER

3

BETTING TERMS

Betting Terms

Poker has special terms used to state each type of action a player may take when it is his turn to act. The standard terms utilized are as follows:

Check   To abstain from betting but continue to stay in contention for the pot because nobody else has yet to bet on that round. Same as pass.

Bet   To make or initiate a wager by putting chips into the pot.

Raise   To make a bet increasing the size of a previous wager on that betting round.

Call   To match the bet of another player. If a player's funds are insufficient to match the entire bet, he may call a portion of it equal to the total amount he has left on the table. Only money or chips on the table play during a hand.

Fold   To discard ones own hand.

CHAPTER

4

CARDS

Cards

Poker is played with one deck of cards with backs of the same color and design and one additional solid cover card. At all times, two decks of cards, a "setup" are maintained for use at each poker table. Each deck maintained at the poker table must be visually distinguishable in some manner from the other deck. While one deck is in use, the other deck must be stored in a designated area.

Each deck maintained at the poker table may be rotated in and out of play. All decks (setups) opened for use on a poker table may be changed at the discretion of management or by the request of a player. In any type of game, players cannot be granted a deck change until at least one hand per player has been dealt. This helps to lessen the amount of down time during a game by needlessly changing a perfectly good deck of cards. Anytime a card or cards are damaged, it will be changed out immediately, regardless of the number of hands played.

Please remember, all poker rules and procedures are established by each casino. House rules **always** prevail over commonly accepted rules and procedures that are in conflict with the established house rules.

CHAPTER

5

PROCEDURES ALL POKER GAMES

Procedures-All Poker Games

Poker is played by a minimum of two players and a maximum number of players that the cards and table comfort will allow (generally a maximum of ten in flop games and eight in stud-type games).

The dealer, when dealing in a casino, will not participate in the actual playing or outcome of the game.

The ranking of suits from highest to lowest is spades, hearts, diamonds and clubs.

Suit ranking is not used to determine the ranking of a poker hand, only for an opening bet as required in stud-type games.

Cards speak. A hand is read by its actual cards and not by the verbal assessment of a player.

A player can only use the money he has on the table at the beginning of the hand. Money can only be increased by the player between hands.

Money can only be removed from the table by a player who is quitting the game. Tipping is not considered removing money from play. A player must quit the game for at least two hours before returning to that respective game with less money or as the house rules dictate.

A joker card dealt is not a playable card. If a joker card is dealt face up it is replaced by the top card in the deck. If a joker card is dealt facedown, the top card of the deck is dealt facedown after the players have received all of their cards. Actually, if it appears in the initial deal, it is a misdeal as it is a fouled deck. If it appears during the course of play, it is considered a boxed card.

A player is not allowed to receive help relative to the play of his hand from anyone during the hand. One player to a hand.

A misdeal can be called for certain irregularities during the initial betting round, unless substantial action has taken place. The following are examples of some irregularities that might be construed as a misdeal. House rules always dictate these generalities.

a. The first card was dealt to the wrong person.
b. The first or second card of the hand has been dealt faceup.
c. A player has been dealt out who is entitled to a hand.
d. Cards have been dealt to an empty seat.
e. Cards have been dealt to a player who is not entitled to a hand.
f. The button was out of position.

   g. Two or more cards were exposed by the dealer.

   h. Two or more boxed cards are found.

An error during a hand can only be corrected as is deemed best by the floor person if substantial action takes place before the error is discovered.

Two players must act to be considered substantial action. This substantial action will require the error to stand and the hand proceed as if an error did not occur. A misdeal generally cannot be declared once substantial action takes place.

All wagers by a player will be placed by the dealer in the designated area of the table known as the pot.

Players may be required to ante or place a blind bet prior to receipt of any cards.

After the dealing and betting has occurred for a pot and there are two or more players still in contention, there will be a showdown to determine which player has the best hand.

The object of the game is for a player to win the pot by making a wager that no other player elects to call or by the player having the most valuable hand at the showdown as determined by the ranking of hands.

The order of showdown is initiated by the player making the final wager. He will be the first player to show his hand with all others following in turn in a clockwise rotation. In a stud game, the showdown is initiated by the player who is high on the board, if there is no final card bet. In flop games, with no river bet, the player to the left of the button would be the first to show his cards.

The dealer must verbalize or physically indicate the action that is occurring at the poker table with regard to the play.

As needed, the dealer will instruct the players of their various turns to act and their various options.

The dealer is required to count the deck stub at least once every down, on a random basis, in order to determine that the correct number of cards is present. If this count reveals an incorrect number of cards, the deck will be removed from the table.

At the completion of the hand, the dealer will award the pot to the winning player. Prior to pushing the pot to the winner, the dealer must first collect the cards from all of the losing players.

All discarded hands must be verified by the dealer for determination of the proper number of cards being returned.

All side pots must be awarded by the dealer before the main pot, in the center of the table, is awarded.

After the pot has been awarded, the dealer will drop the house rake.

Players are permitted to check and then raise a bettor.

It is considered a check if a player taps the table or makes a gesture that can be interpreted as passing or makes a verbal declaration that he checks or passes.

It is a player's responsibility to protect his hand at all times. It is possible for a dealer to accidentally muck a player's unprotected hand.

It is a player's responsibility to protest his right to act by immediately objecting if the dealer has passed him in error. Once substantial action occurs, the player will lose his right to initiate action. If facing a bet and four players have acted, the player will have a dead hand.

A dead hand is declared when any part of the hand hits the muck or is thrown in another player's hand either faceup or facedown and the cards are intermingled to the extent that they cannot be properly identified.

A hand may be retrieved when it has caused no action by another player and has not yet been mucked.

A player who has been dealt into the hand may request to see a called hand that is discarded after the final round of betting is completed.

A time request may be called by a player when he feels another player is taking too long to act. The player will receive one minute and ten seconds to act. At the end of the minute, the player will receive a ten second countdown. If the player has not acted, his hand will be considered dead.

Players can agree to split or chop the blinds. When an agreement is made to do so, it must be consistent. It cannot be changed hand by hand.

Players may agree to split the pot prior to the winning hand being declared; unless there is a specific rule of the cardroom prohibiting it and there are no objections from the other players.

A player may or may not read at the table. It is a policy that is made by the management of each respective cardroom.

A player may or may not eat at the table. It is a policy that is made by the management of each respective cardroom.

If a player quits the game and then returns to the game in less than two hours, it does not create a new play session. The player must buy in for at least the amount equal to his money on the table when he quit the game.

A player has the right to know how much money in play another player has available. If necessary, a count of a player's money can be requested, if this information is vital to the play.

A player may only add chips to his table bankroll between hands. The buy-in requirement only applies to new players or a player who went all-in and lost the hand.

Side bets are not allowed if a player's table bankroll is used for the bet.

A completed hand occurs when the dealer starts the shuffle for the next hand. A shuffle is begun by the first riffle of the cards.

If a player makes a miscall bet by calling only the original bet because he is unaware that a raise took place, the player may withdraw the wager or increase it to the size of the raise. If another player acts behind him, he must leave the call in and forfeit his hand or complete the bet.

A string bet is not allowed and occurs when the player puts the amount of the call into the pot, without making a verbal declaration of a raise, and returns to his bankroll to add more chips to the bet.

A raise made with a continuous motion is a legitimate bet.

A player may make a verbal declaration as to his intention to his betting action.

A player who initiates action out of turn will be required to take that action when it is his turn to act. If the action in front of the player who had action out of turn is equal to or greater that his announced action, his announced action is then considered null and void.

A misdeal occurs in all games when the first or second card off the deck is exposed.

If a player is dealt more or less cards than his game requires, and it is discovered before action is taken, it is a misdeal. If two or more players act before it is discovered, the player has a fouled hand.

It is the players' responsibility to protect their hands at all times. Occasionally, dealers unintentionally will reach to kill winning hands that they have misread. A tabled hand, (a hand placed face up on the table), cannot be killed.

A boxed card or exposed card is a card face up in the deck.

    a. If two or more boxed cards are found in the deck before any action is taken, it constitutes a misdeal.

    b. A boxed card never plays in any game and is always treated as a scrap of paper and replaced by the next card in the deck.

A player's hand becomes a dead hand when any of the following occurs:

a. You announce that you are folding when facing a bet.

b. You throw your hand away in a forward motion causing a player behind you to act.

c. When facing a bet in stud, you turn your upcards facedown or mix your upcards and downcards together.

d. You exceed the specified time when you have the clock on you.

e. Your hand does not contain the proper number of cards for that particular game.

f. Cards thrown into another player's hand are dead, whether they are faceup or facedown.

g. Cards thrown into the muck may be ruled dead. A discarded hand, that is identifiable, may be retrieved from the muck if it was folded as a result of false information given to the player or other irregularity as deemed appropriate by the floor person.

CHAPTER

6

GAME PROCEDURES

Game Procedures

It is the responsibility of the player not to discard his hand before he is completely satisfied that he has a losing hand.

In disputes in which a ruling, interpretation, clarification or intervention is required, the decision of the poker shift supervisor is final.

Players are required to keep all cards dealt to them in full view of the dealer and players at all times.

At the showdown, a winning hand must be clearly displayed in its entirety and properly identified. The player initiating the final wager should be the first player to show his hand at the showdown with all other players showing their hand in a clockwise rotation. Players holding losing hands may concede their rights to the pot and discard their hands.

When a misdeal occurs, the cards are returned to the dealer for a redeal. The following errors create a misdeal:

    a. Failure to shuffle and cut the cards.
    b. Dealing to an incorrect starting position, if substantial action has not taken place.
    c. If more than one boxed card is found in the deck, provided substantial action has not taken place.
    d. Failure to deal to an eligible seated player, if substantial action has not taken place.

If an ineligible player is mistakenly dealt in, only those cards dealt to that player is discarded, that hand declared dead, and the round of play continues.

If at any time during play, missing cards are discovered or additional cards are found, the hand is called dead. All gaming chips in the pot are returned to the appropriate players and the deck is replaced. The hand is considered no action.

If a player folds his hand after making a forced bet, blind bet, or on a round of checking, that player's position will continue to receive a card until there is a subsequent wager at the table.

CHAPTER

7

CARD PROCEDURES

Card Procedures

After receiving two decks of cards at the table (called a setup), the dealer will inspect the cards.

The cards will be spread out, face up, on the table for visual inspection by the dealer. The players are encouraged to visually inspect them as well. The cards will be spread out by suit and in sequence. Then, the cards will be spread facedown to insure that they are of matching backs and no obvious imperfections.

Prior to the commencement of play and in the presence of a minimum of two players, one of the following two methods must be used:

1. The cards from each deck will be visually inspected at the table; each deck will be separately turned facedown at the table. They will then be mixed thoroughly, washed (scrambled), and replaced into the stack for dealing. One deck will be used for play and the second deck stored in the table rack for later use.

2. The dealer makes available one deck of cards for visual inspection by a minimum of two players. The dealer will then wash (scramble), shuffle, and cut only the deck intended for immediate use and maintain the second deck in the table rack for later use.

CHAPTER

8

SHUFFLE AND CUT PROCEDURE

Shuffle and Cut Procedure

Immediately prior to commencement of play and after the completion of each round of play, the dealer will shuffle the cards so that they are randomly intermixed. The shuffle will be wash (scramble), as is determined by the prevailing house rule, shuffle, strip three times, shuffle, shuffle. Also acceptable is shuffle, shuffle, box, shuffle.

After the cards have been shuffled and placed on the table in front of the dealer, the dealer will cut the deck, using one hand, by placing a top portion of the deck on top of a cover card and then place the remaining stack of cards on top. The top portion of the deck placed on the cut card must consist of at least ten cards. The cover card should always be placed in front of the stack of cards prior to the cut of the cards by the dealer.

If there is no gaming activity at the poker table, each deck of cards should be spread out on the table, face up if the decks have not been used or facedown if the cards have been used. If the games is to be down for more than a few moments, the dealer should always make the setups back to allow for a new inspection when the games starts up again.

CHAPTER

9

WAGER RULES

Wager Rules

Only players who are seated at the poker table or who have requested a hand may be permitted to receive cards in a live game, and participate in each betting round. In some cardrooms, any player who has posted a blind will continue to be dealt in until he misses a blind. This generally is in a higher limit game.

Depending upon the particular type of poker game being dealt, a player may be required to do one of the following:

    a. Post an ante prior to receiving any cards.
    b. Post a predetermined blind bet prior to receiving any cards.
    c. Place a forced bet to initiate a betting round based on that player's upcard.

Once a hand has commenced, a player may only participate in the wagering on that round of play with the gaming chips or currency that has already been placed on the poker table in front of him.

Currency available for use may be utilized to initiate, call, or raise a wager. Currency should be converted into gaming chips by the dealer as soon as possible. Some houses allow the cash to be played and remain in the pot.

A player with sufficient gaming chips and currency available to participate initially in a round of play, but who depletes these funds prior to completion of that round of play, will be deemed to be all-in.

An all-in player will retain financial interest in the outcome of the hand, but only up to the amount of the pot to which that player has contributed.

An all-in player will continue to receive cards to which that player would normally be entitled.

Wagering will continue among the other players by generating a separate secondary pot, which only those active players will be eligible to win. This is called a side pot and will consist of the bets above and beyond the amount that the all-in player placed.

A verbal announcement of fold, check, call, raise, or an announcement of a specific size wager will be binding on the player.

A player who announces a wager or raise of a certain amount but places a different amount of gaming chips in the pot will be required to correct his wager to the stated amount.

A player shall be considered to have placed a wager if the player does one of the following:

1. Releases gaming chips into the pot.
2. Releases gaming chips at a sufficient distance from the player and in the direction of the pot to make it reasonably obvious that it is intended as a wager.

A player who puts the proper amount of gaming chips into the pot to call the wager, without indicating a raise may not add additional chips to the pot for a raise. String bets are not allowed and depending on local rules, may or may not be called by the dealer. It is always correct for a player to call a string bet when the dealer has not.

It is the dealer's responsibility to ensure that no player touches any of the gaming chips once placed into the pot.

A player who puts a single chip into the pot that is larger than the bet is assumed to have only called the bet, unless he verbally announced his intention to raise. The dealer should not ask the player if he is raising the pot. Simply, an oversize chip without comment is merely a call.

Check and raise is permitted, unless otherwise specified.

If there are three or more players, there will be a maximum of four raises, plus the original bet per betting round. This is optional and depends on the house rule.

In a heads-up situation, there are no limits to the number of raises. A betting round must begin heads up for it to be unlimited raising. Some house rules allow unlimited betting if it becomes heads-up before the betting has been capped.

Half Bet Rule

A player, who has half or more of the required bet but not enough for a full bet or raise, can bet that amount. It is treated as a full bet. The next player can fold, call the half bet, complete the bet or raise the full bet.

If a player has less than half the amount bet, he may call for that amount. It is considered action only and does not constitute a bet or a raise. It does not reopen the betting to a player who already has acted. The other players that have not had a chance to act on their hands have three options. They may fold; call the amount bet or raise the full bet.

A player who adds chips to the amount required to call a bet that equals or exceeds one and one half times the required amount will have his wager considered a raise. The following players may fold, call the amount bet, or call the amount bet and make a full raise.

Full Bet Rule

Depending on specific house rules, anything less than a full bet or raise does not re-open the betting.

Due to the simplicity of this rule, it is now being implemented in many casinos.

CHAPTER

10

EMPLOYEE RULES

Employee Rules

All rules and regulations of the casino and the poker room must be observed by every employee. Failure to do so may mean suspension or termination.

All employees must sign in and clock in or follow other required rules as set forth by the property.

All employees must have a current telephone number or other contact information on file in the poker room.

An employee calling in sick or having any other problems that causes him to be unable to show up for his scheduled work time, must call in at least two hours before his shift start and speak to the poker room shift manager on duty at the time.

Employees have the responsibility to check their work schedules for changes.

Employees are not allowed to receive or make telephone calls unless it is an emergency. In an emergency situation, permission must be given by the shift manager before receiving or making the telephone call. Other house rules may apply.

Each poker room employee must wear a name tag.

Employees are not allowed to borrow or loan money to customers at any time.

Back and/or neck massages are not to be given by an employee to customers or other employees in the poker room.

Employees are not allowed to have anything in their mouth while in the poker room.

Employees are not allowed to order or drink alcoholic beverages while on duty.

Dealers are not allowed to make decisions on the game. A supervisor or shift manager must make all decisions.

A shift manager or floor person is the only person allowed to make game changes or alter the structure of the game.

A supervisor must be present at the start of a game. When a new game is started, the dealer and the table bank must already be in place.

Racks must be checked by the incoming dealer at the start of each down according to the policy of the cardroom.

Racks must be checked by a supervisor on a regular basis.

All fills must be made between hands. The money and the respective lammers (marker buttons) must be spread on the table for review by surveillance.

Game security is the number one priority. The cards and the table rack must never be left unattended.

CHAPTER

11

RAKE

Rake

The rake should not exceed 10% of the total wagered and called in the hand or the declared maximum rake posted at the table.

The rake must be taken from the pot in a consistent manner.

The rake must be placed in a designated rake circle or drop slot where it will remain until a winner is declared and the pot pushed. The rake will then be dropped in the drop box. The rake must be clearly visible to all players until it is dropped.

If the table is equipped with a cover over the drop slot, the drop box cover will serve as the drop circle.

Under or over raking is not an acceptable practice.

Using seven-card stud as an example, the rake procedure is as follows:

Assume a $1-3 game and there are six players in the game. The opening bet is the only forced bet in the game. The low card starts the betting with $.50. Each of the players calls making it $3.00 in the pot. A 10% rake would be $.25. Quarters are the smallest denomination in play, so $.30 could not be raked. In a cardroom using nothing smaller than half dollars, there would not be a rake at this point. A dealer may never round up. This would be taken from the pot after the next round of cards is dealt and the highest current hand is determined to begin the action.

From this point on, we will use a running total to determine the total rake that should be taken directly from the pot.

We had $3.00 in the pot and the next betting round was by five players. A $1.00 bet with four callers making it $5.00 betting round. We now have $8.00 in the pot. Our total rake should be $.75. The dealer must now take $.50 from the pot.

A running total means adding the last round of betting to what was previously bet.

The rake should never have four quarters in the rake circle. The rake total should be changed to the highest denomination chip.

CHAPTER

12

RACK CHIP FILLS

Rack Chip Fills

When the rack starts to get low on chips or coins, call for a chip fill. Do not leave the rack short for the next dealer.

When getting a fill, count out all of the cash in the rack.

Money for a fill must be counted in full view on the table. The chip runner or supervisor making the fill must be present when the dealer counts the money for the fill. Lammers are then placed on the table next to the rack to verify the amount of cash being used for the fill. The lammers must be in clear view for verification by surveillance.

Fills must be verified by the dealer, in the presence of the chip runner or supervisor, before being placed in the rack.

A full stack should be broken down and then matched to the other full stacks. Short stacks should be broken down and counted.

If an error occurs in the fill, the dealer should not accept the fill. The lammers will remain on the table until the proper fill is received.

After the proper fill is received and verified, the lammers are returned to the table rack or the chip runner depending on the procedures used by the casino.

CHAPTER

13

CHIP RUNNER

Chip Runner

The chip runner will try to make all table game fills.

The chip runner will also assist the brush person as is possible and needed with seating players, player requests as well as chip requirements.

The chip runner should periodically check the dealer's racks for necessary fills as time allows before a fill is called.

A fill is never to be made during a hand.

Fills should never be left on a table unattended.

The chip runner cannot pick up money or chips from a table until he verifies that the dealer has the proper amount of lammers in view on the table. The chip runner must never reach into the rack to get cash. This must be counted on the felt, in full view, before being handed to the runner.

The chip runner cannot pick up lammers from the table. They must be picked up by the dealer. The dealer will either place the lammers in the chip rack or hand them to the chip runner after the chip purchase transaction is completed. As procedures dictates, in some cardrooms, the lammers will go directly back into the dealer chip tray.

When lammers are placed on the table by the dealer they represent money for a fill. They must be spread out so that all lammers are clearly visible for the supervisor and surveillance.

The chip runner should acknowledge a dealer who has announced an open seat or has requested a new setup or a fill. The proper way to do this is to call out "thank you table x". A dealer should only call a second time if enough time has elapsed without an acknowledgement or the dealer is certain his call was not heard.

CHAPTER

14

BRUSH PERSON

Brush Person

The brush person is responsible for the keeping of all player lists.

The brush person will make announcements for all poker games.

The brush person should not combine games unless this has been approved by a supervisor or shift manager.

The brush person should keep the games balanced. If all the tables are balanced the original game should be filled first.

A game plaque is to be placed on the table at the start of the game. The plaque must be clearly visible to the patrons.

A table must be opened with a dealer and bank before the game is started. This should be done as soon as there are players on the list. The brush person should notify the supervisor that the table should be opened and operational as soon as possible.

The brush person should not make any game decisions. Refer all decisions to a supervisor or shift manager.

Brush person should acknowledge a dealer who has announced an open seat; fill player's chips, a rack, or setup.

    a. Brush persons response is "Thank you".

    b. A dealer should not have to announce more than once what is needed at his table.

The brush person should immediately clean the poker table when a player leaves the table.

CHAPTER

15

DEALING PROCEDURES

Dealing Procedures

The dealer should clock and sign in 20 minutes prior to the start of his shift. (This rule may vary according to a specific house rule.)

A dealer returning from a break should be in position behind the dealer being relieved one minute early. Again, this is subject to house rules. Many cardrooms have the dealer push one minute early for each table in the lineup being pushed.

The dealer being relieved must have the bank in order for the incoming dealer so that it is easy to verify.

The dealer being relieved should inform the incoming dealer of any special conditions relative to the game. These could include pointing out any player in absent button jeopardy or who has had a short buy in or who has had a warning for abuse of any sort. It is also correct to inform the dealer of novice players at the game who might be in need of additional assistance.

The shuffling procedure must follow the prescribed house shuffle. It must not deviate from the standard house shuffle.

The dealer will use one hand to cut the deck. The direction of the cut is straight away from the dealer. Both hands must be completely free from the deck before the cut is started. The free hand may not touch the deck until the cutting hand has rejoined the two stubs. The free hand should not block the view of the cutting procedure. The deck should not be left in the half cut position for any reason. If a cut deck cannot be picked up for any reason, it is to be capped.

The top half of the deck is put onto a cover-card when the deck is cut so that the bottom card will be covered at all times. At least 10 cards must be cut from either end of the deck.

The stub of the deck is to be kept squared and compacted throughout the deal. If it becomes necessary for the dealer to square up the deck, the dealer should tap the edge of the deck from the rear, using his thumb or the palm of his free hand. The dealer should not cover the top of the deck with his other hand or any fingers.

The top of the deck must never be obscured from the view of any of the players or turned downward towards the table. The deck is never to be rolled at any time.

The dealer must place the burn cards under chips in the pot to keep them separate from the discards. The burn cards should remain in place until the last card has been dealt. At this time, the deck is to be dropped and spread. Once the final betting round has commenced, the burn cards, muck, and deck stub may be intermingled unless this is contrary to house rules.

A burn card may not be shown to a player. If a burn card is exposed to a player, it must then be shown to all the players remaining in the hand. This is similar to the rule prohibiting rabbit hunting and is never allowed.

Discards should be kept in a loose pile several inches from and toward the left side of the dealer's chip rack. This could be reversed if the dealer is left-handed.

Players may not look in the discard pile at any time.

The dealer should not square up the discards pile until after all cards are taken in at the end of the hand. The dealer's free hand must not rest on the discards.

The dealer should deal the cards so that they reach the player.

The dealer should hold the deck as level as possible at all times. The deck may not be rolled at any time.

Any time after the cut, if the dealer must place the deck down; such as when counting a stack of bills, the deck must be capped by a marker button.

If cards are exposed by a dealer or by a player, the exposed cards are to be announced and shown to the entire table.

The dealer is responsible for giving information about exposed cards to all of the players. Additional cards, beyond the actual cards exposed, should never be shown.

Wagers are not to be brought into the pot by the dealer until the betting round is completed.

The dealer should announce to the players any time a bet placed in front of a player is not the actual size of the previous bet. The dealer should announce, "call" if an oversize chip is put into the pot without comment by the player making the bet.

The dealer is responsible for making sure the amount of chips placed in the pot is the actual amount represented by the bettor.

All large bets must be counted by the dealer. Stacks of six or more chips should be broken down and counted.

The dealer should inform the players when an all-in bet is made.

The dealer is to take all discarded hands and muck them immediately.

A hand discarded out of turn should be mucked immediately. The offending player should be told that the action had not yet reached him and he should be requested to act in turn in the future.

A discarded hand, at the showdown, should be placed in the muck, thus killing the hand.

In stud, a player who turns his upcards facedown or mixes his upcards and down-cards together has folded his hand and the dealer should muck the hand.

A discarded hand may be returned to the player if it has not hit the muck under the following circumstances:

a. The player thinks he won the pot and there is still a live hand out.
b. A player already in for a bet incorrectly thinks he owes more money and discards his hand.

The dealer should make a general announcement at the showdown requesting the hands to be shown.

The dealer should not ask a specific player to show his hand unless it is necessary to designate who is legally obligated to show his hand first.

The dealer must request players contending for a side pot to show their hands first, before the player(s) contending for the main pot only.

The dealer should make sure all cards of the winning hand are shown before awarding the pot.

The winning hand should remain face up until the pot has been awarded. All losing hands should be mucked before awarding the pot.

When the deal is over, the dealer should place the burn cards and the unused stub in the discard pile. Discarded hands are to be slid into the middle of the discard pile; they should not be placed on top. This insures a better scramble of the cards.

In games that use a button, push the pot to the winner before moving the button.

CHAPTER

16

MISSED BIG BLIND

Missed Big Blind

When a player missed his big blind, the dealer must place a missed big blind button in front of the players place at the table.

Upon returning to the games, the player must do one of the following:

1. Wait until the button comes around to where his position is the big blind.
2. Wait until the button passes him. At this time, he puts up a combination of the total of the big blind and the small blind. The small blind is placed in the center of the table and it is a dead blind. The amount of the big blind remains in front of the player and it is a live bet. The player can raise, check, or call the action to him.

CHAPTER

17

MISSED SMALL BLIND

Missed Small Blind

When a player misses his small blind, the dealer places a missed small blind button in front of the players place at the table.

When the player returns to the game, he must do one of the following:

1. Wait until the button comes around to the player again and he is in the big blind position.
2. He may be dealt in immediately by posting the small blind. The blind is dead and goes into the center of the table and has no value towards the player's action in the pot.

CHAPTER

18

GENERAL BUTTON PROCEDURES

General Button Procedures

There are basically two different systems used to determine the placement of the blinds, the forward moving button or the dead button.

The dead button system is the simplest. It is the system used in tournaments and in most open games.

Forward moving button: The dealer button always moves forward to the next active player regardless if the player has previously posted the small or big blind. However, each player must, in turn, post his small and big blind.

As an example; if player #2 is the button and player #3 posts the small blind and player #4 posts the big blind, the hand proceeds in the normal manner.

On the following hand, player #3 quits the game. The button would then move forward to player #4. He would have the button and is required to put in his live small blind. Player #5 would put in his big blind and player #6 would also put in a big blind.

On the following hand, the button would again move forward to player #5. He would now put in his live small blind and player #6 would put in his live small blind. Player #7 would now put in his live big blind.

On the following hand, the button would again move forward to player #6, who has already posted his small and big blind. Player #7 would put in his live small blind and player #8 would put in his big blind.

At this point, the button and the blinds are back in the normal sequence.

As is demonstrated by the above example, the forward moving button system can be complicated and therefore, the simpler dead button rule is now being used in most cardrooms.

Dead button: Each active player must post in turn, the small blind and then the big blind before the dealer button moves to them.

As and example; if player #2 is the button and player #3 posts the small blind and player #4 places the big blind, the hand proceeds as normal.

On the following hand, player #3 quits the game. The button would not move to player #4 at this time because he has not placed his small blind yet.

The button would move to the empty seat of player #3. Player #4 would now place his small blind and player #5 would place his big blind.

On the following hand, the button would now move to player #4. Player #5 would place his small blind and player #6 would place his big blind. The button and the blinds are already back in the proper sequence.

The dead button system only requires that one small blind and one big blind are posted by an active player in proper turn.

However, this system could cause the dealer button to move to two dead positions in a row, but there would still only be one small blind and one big blind.

White button: A white button indicates an absent player. The incoming dealer will place a white button at the seat of the absent player when the dealer deals the first hand of each down.

A player receiving two white buttons will be picked up after fifteen minutes have passed. Their chips will be counted by a supervisor, and verified by the dealer, and placed in an envelope. The actual time they were picked up should be indicated on the envelope.

If a player goes broke and locks up a seat, the white button rule will be used.

If a player requests a dinner break, he will be allowed to receive three white buttons and fifteen minutes before being picked up.

If a player is picked up and returns within fifteen minutes of the time he is picked up, he will be placed at the top of the player list.

This white button rule applies to all games.

Specific house rules may alter the times allowed.

Yellow button: When a seat becomes available, a yellow *reserve* seat button will be placed at the available seat and the supervisor notified.

Green button: A green button is used as a *missed* big blind indicator. It is placed at the player's place on the table when the player misses his big blind.

Brown button: A brown button is used as a *missed* small blind indicator. This button is placed at the player's place on the table when he has missed his small blind.

CHAPTER

19

KILL POTS

Kill Pots

A kill pot means the size of the betting structure doubles following the hand that a kill was achieved.

A kill can be a full kill or a half kill. This is an option decided upon by the players or by a specific house rule. (House rules always prevail).

A full kill means the betting structure is doubled and a half-kill means the betting structure is increased one and a half times the normal betting structure.

A kill is created in a straight high or low game when a player wins two consecutive pots. The pot size required is determined by a specific house rule.

A kill button is used to indicate when a player wins the first leg of a kill. This is called a "leg-up".

In a straight high or straight low game, the player that has a leg-up must win the second pot to create a kill. If he splits the pot, the next hand continues as a pot with the player having just a leg-up.

If the player has already created the kill pot and then splits the following hand, he again is the "kill" player.

A specific house rule could also be established that requires a player to win the pot in its entirety in order to create a kill.

This would mean that if a pot is split by any of the players at any time, the kill is neutral.

In a high-low split game, the player must "scoop" the pot in order to create a "kill" pot. If the player has a leg-up or is the "kill", he still must scoop the pot or the kill factor is again neutral.

Most casinos have specific house rules relative to the minimum amount of money that must be in the pot to create a kill.

In a "flop" game, the flop must also occur in order to create a legup or a new kill. However if a player is the "kill" and the kill is not called before the flop and a flop does not take place, the player will continue as the kill. If there is action before the flop and then a flop does not take place and a player, other than the player with the kill wins the pot, the kill factor than becomes neutral.

In a kill pot, depending on the house rule, the player posting the kill either acts in turn or he acts last.

If the house rule dictates that he acts last, he will do so unless there is a raise in front of him and then he acts in turn.

There is only one kill bet made in a hand. A live straddle is not allowed in a kill hand.

If the player with a leg-up leaves the game, he will have a leg-up upon his return.

If a player has the kill and leaves the game, he must either post the amount of the kill in the pot or he must post the amount of the kill before he is allowed to participate in ANY game. A kill is money that is owed to the pot.

If the player posting the kill wins the pot, he again must post the amount of the required kill.

A new player to the game is not entitled to participate in the kill pot. He must wait until the next hand that is not a kill pot.

CHAPTER

20

TEXAS HOLD'EM

Texas Hold'em

Texas Hold'em is a poker game using 5 to 7 cards to make the best possible high hand.

Each player receives two cards in his hand and five community cards on the board.

Any combination of these seven cards may be used to make his hand.

It is permissible for a player to play the five community cards on the board as his hand. He may not discard his cards before declaring that he is playing the cards on the board. If he discards his hand prior to making the declaration to play the board, his hand is considered a dead hand.

A small blind and a big blind are used to start each hand of play. The small blind is made by the player in the first position to the left of the designated dealer button. The big blind is made by the player seated two positions to the left of the designated dealer button.

A player is not allowed to enter the game between the blinds. He may enter the game on his big blind or by waiting until the dealer button passes him.

Depending on the house rule, it is permissible to enter the game by posting (putting in) the big blind. If the player elects to post the big blind it is considered a live bet and the player will act in the regular rotation of the game.

If a player misses his big blind, he can return to the game by waiting for his proper turn to place the big blind or by putting in his big blind, which is a live bet.

If the player missed only his small blind, he may wait until the button passes him and post the small blind, which is a dead bet.

An extra live blind may only be made by the player left of the big blind. This bet is called a live straddle. It must be double the size of the big blind.

When there are only two players in the game, the small blind is on the button.

When a player changes his seat three or more active players to the left of the big blind, he must wait for the big blind or post a live bet equal to the size of the big blind.

A player in the small blind position that changes his seat must post a live small blind from his new seat.

When a player's holecard is exposed by the dealer, it must be replaced. The player may not elect to keep the card. The dealer will complete the deal and then replace the exposed card with the top card of the deck. The exposed card will then be used as the first burn card.

If the dealer exposes either of the first two cards being dealt, it will cause a misdeal.

If the dealer exposes either of the cards being dealt to the player on the button, the player may not elect to keep the card nor will it create a misdeal. The dealer will complete the deal and then replace the exposed card with the top card of the deck. The exposed card will then be used as the first burn card.

House rule here is important because some casinos prefer to have an exposed card to the button create a misdeal.

If the dealer exposes any two holecards, the deal will be considered a misdeal.

If the dealer flops too many cards, the entire flop will be taken back and reshuffled with the deck stub only. The discards and the burn card are not reshuffled. The dealer will not burn another card. He will only replace the flop with the proper number of cards.

If a dealer burns and turns before the betting is complete the following procedure must be used:

a) Before the flop: the dealer will remove the flopped cards and have the players complete the betting. He will then reshuffle the flopped cards with the stub and then re-flop the cards. He will not reshuffle the burn card nor will he burn another card before the re-flop.

b) On the turn: If the turn card is put up before the betting is complete, it will not play. The betting will be completed. After the betting is completed, another card from the deck is burned and the next card is used as the turn card. The misdealt turn card is held to the side until the betting for this round is complete. When the betting round is completed, the misdealt card is placed in the deck stub and reshuffled. The burn cards and the discards are not reshuffled. The dealer will then place the next card from the deck on the board as the fifth card without burning a card. The betting round will again resume.

c) On the river: If the river card is dealt before the betting is completed, it will be placed in the deck stub. The betting is completed. The deck stub is then reshuffled and the fifth (river) card is placed on the board and the final round of betting is completed. The burn card and the discards are not reshuffled.

CHAPTER

21

SEVEN CARD STUD

Seven Card Stud

All seven card stud games should be restricted to eight players.

All players usually are required to post an ante.

Starting to the left of the dealer, two rounds are dealt facedown and one round is dealt faceup to each of the players.

After each player receives three cards the first round of betting takes place.

The player with the lowest upcard is required to make the opening bet.

An ace is considered a high card for the opening bet.

In the event two or more cards of the same rank are dealt, the cards are then ranked by suit. The lowest ranking card by suit will start the first round of betting.

After the player with the lowest card places the forced bet, the following players may fold, call or raise the bet.

When the first round of betting is completed, the dealer will burn the top card of the deck and then deal another round of cards faceup to the remaining players in the hand.

The player with the highest hand showing is required to bet or check.

Beginning with this betting round, if two or more hands are of equal ranking, the player closest to the left of the dealer will act first.

The dealer must burn the top card of the deck prior to dealing each round of cards.

The dealer will deal the next two rounds of cards faceup. A betting round will follow each round of cards dealt.

The final round of cards will be dealt facedown to each remaining player followed by a round of betting.

After all the bets are acted upon in the final round of betting, if more than one player remains, a showdown of the hands will determine the winner.

Each remaining player in the hand must form his best five-card hand from the seven cards dealt to him.

All seven cards must be exposed.

The player with the highest-ranking five-card hand is the winner.

If a tie exists between the players, the excess is given to the player with the highest-ranking hand using all seven cards.

In a structured game, if a player has a pair on fourth street, he will have an option to bet either the minimum or the maximum amount.

In a structured game, the player with the highest hand on fifth street must either check or bet the maximum amount.

A player must have all seven cards to be eligible to win the pot. any other number of cards will constitute a dead hand.

A player who calls a bet on the river and is beaten by another players up cards is not entitled to a refund. It is the player's responsibility to read the cards on the board.

A player may not rearrange the order of his upcards. He must leave them in the order in which they were dealt.

If a player picks up his upcards without calling the bet, he has a dead hand. A player that calls the final bet may pick up his hand without being penalized.

If a player puts in his ante and is not dealt a hand, it is a misdeal. If substantial action takes place prior to recognizing the error, he will receive his ante back and the hand will proceed.

If the dealer deals a card to a dead seat and it is realized before he deals to the next player, the card is moved to the correct player. If additional cards are dealt and the mistake cannot be corrected, it is a misdeal.

When a dealer burns and deals a card before the round of betting is completed, the entire round must be eliminated. The dealer will burn a card for each remaining player in the hand. The entire round is then placed in the discards. The dealer then burns a card and deals a new round of cards.

If a players first or second card is dealt faceup, his third card is to be dealt facedown. If the same player receives two cards faceup, he has a dead hand. The player must then receive his ante back. He does not have the option to play the hand.

If there are not enough cards in the deck to finish the final round, the dealer will burn a card and deal a community card that is used by all the remaining players. The player who was high on the previous round will initiate the action on this round of betting.

If there are not enough cards to complete the round and some players have already received cards, the cards remaining in the deck stub and the burn cards must be used to form a new deck. These cards are shuffled, cut, a card burned and then dealt to the remaining players. The last card of the deck is not to be used.

If the first player receives his last card faceup, all remaining players must receive their last card faceup. The player that initiated the betting on the previous round again initiates the betting.

If a player who is not in the first position has his last card turned up by mistake, the player has the option to declare himself all-in and play for what is in the pot. He may also elect to have full action on the hand. The player whose hand was high on sixth street will start the betting action.

If a river card is dealt off the table, it is used but it is treated as an exposed down card.

If the cards are dealt to the players out of the proper sequence, the cards should be moved to the proper position to correct the error. When the down cards are dealt out of the proper sequence and there is no way to correct the problem, the players must accept the cards as dealt.

CHAPTER

22

SEVEN CARD STUD HI/LO SPLIT EIGHT OR BETTER

Seven Card Stud High-Low Split Eight or Better

All seven card stud high-low games should be restricted to eight players.

All players are required to post an ante.

Starting with the player to the left of the dealer, two rounds are dealt facedown and one round is dealt faceup.

After each player receives three cards, the first round of betting takes place.

The player with the lowest upcard is required to make the opening bet.

Upon the completion of the first betting round, the dealer will burn the top card of the deck and then deal another round of cards faceup to the remaining players in the hand. The next round of betting will then begin.

The player with the highest-ranking hand showing is required to bet or check.

If two or more hands are of equal value, beginning with this betting round, the player closest to the left of the dealer will act first.

The dealer will continue to deal the next two rounds of cards faceup and the final round of cards facedown. The dealer will burn the top card of the deck before dealing each round of cards.

A betting round will follow each round of cards received by the remaining players.

Each player remaining in the game will form his best five-card hand from the seven cards dealt to him.

In seven-card stud eight-or-better, a player may form two different hands of five cards from his seven cards.

Each player is entitled to contend for both the high and the low portion of the pot, if a low hand qualifies.

A winning low hand is made up of five cards that does not contain a nine, ten, jack, queen or king.

An ace may be used as a low ranking card to qualify as a low hand and as a high ranking card in his high hand. The ace may be used both ways in the same hand.

A player may use the same five cards for the both high and low end of the pot as long as none of the cards are higher than an eight. A straight or flush does not affect a players' low hand.

The player with the lowest qualified hand will divide the pot equally with the high hand winner of the pot.

If a tie exists between the players with the high hand, the excess chip is given to the player with the highest-ranking high card by using all seven cards.

If a tie exists between the players with the low hand, the excess is given to the player with the lowest ranking card by using all seven cards.

In the event that none of the player's hands qualifies as a low hand, the entire pot is won by the player with the highest hand.

In all stud games, a player must have all seven cards to be eligible to win the pot. If a player does not have seven cards, his hand is declared a dead hand.

CHAPTER

23

OMAHA HIGH POKER

Omaha High Poker

Omaha rules and procedures are very similar to that used in Hold'em, except that Omaha is played with each player having four cards in his hand.

However, two cards (and only two cards) must be used from the player's down cards in combination with three of the community cards on the board. No other combination of cards is allowed to be used to make a hand.

The maximum number of players at the table is optional. The norm is nine or ten players.

A button is used to designate the dealer's position.

The player to the immediate left of the button places the small blind and the player to the immediate left of the small blind places the big blind.

The dealer will deal four cards facedown, one card at a time, in rotation, to each player. The player to the immediate left of the dealer button receives the first card and the player with the button receives the last cards.

After each player receives his four down cards the first betting round begins. The players to the left of the big blind have the option to fold, call or raise the bet. The option to raise the bet or check the bet will also apply to the player who posted the big blind.

After the betting round is completed, the dealer will burn the top card and deal three community cards. The dealer will turn the community cards faceup and place them in the center of the table.

The next betting round will commence with the player to the immediate left of the dealer button having the option to check or bet. The following players may fold, call or raise the bet or, if no bet was made, the player may make an opening bet or check.

At the completion of the betting round, the dealer will burn a card from the top of the deck and deal another card, faceup, to the right of the community cards.

The next betting round begins, following the same procedure as in the previous round of betting.

When the betting round is completed, the dealer will again burn the top card of the deck and deal the fifth and final card, faceup, to the right of the community cards in the center of the table.

The final round of betting takes place.

In Omaha high, the highest five cards, using the above card combination, wins the pot.

In the event of a tied hand, the odd chip is awarded to the player closest to the left of the dealer button.

CHAPTER

24

OMAHA EIGHT OR BETTER HI/LOW SPLIT

Omaha Eight or Better Hi/Low Split

The basic rules and procedures for Omaha Eight or Better is the same as that of straight Omaha High.

Naturally, there are specific rules used to govern the low hands and the effect a qualified low hand has on the outcome of the hand.

Omaha eight-or-better is played with each player having four cards in his hand.

The player must use two cards from his hand in combination with three of the five community cards to make a high hand and two cards from his hand to make a low-hand.

A player may form two different five card hands to compete for both the high and the low end of the pot.

A player may use any two cards from his hand to make a high hand and any two cards to make a low hand. In fact, a card or both cards may be used to make the high hand and the low hand.

An ace may be used as a low card and again as a high card in the same hand.

In order for a hand to qualify for the low end of the pot, it must be made up of two cards from the players hand and three community cards with all of the five cards being an eight or lower.

The pot is divided equally between the player with the highest ranking hand and the player with the lowest, qualified low hand.

If the amount cannot be divided equally between the players with the winning high and the winning low hand, the excess amount is awarded to the player with the high hand.

In a split between the players in either high or low, the odd chip is awarded to the player closest to the left of the dealer button.

CHAPTER

25

PINEAPPLE HOLD'EM

Pineapple Hold'em

All of the basic rules and procedures of Hold'em also apply to Pineapple Hold'em, with the exception being that each player is dealt three (rather than two) cards before the flop of the first three community cards.

After each player receives three cards, a preflop round of betting takes place.

After the preflop round of betting, each player must discard one card from his hand. If a player does not discard one card prior to the flop, his hand must be declared a dead hand.

It is the player's responsibility to discard a card before the flop.

As in a normal Hold'em game, any combination of five cards may be used to form a high hand.

CHAPTER

26

RAZZ

Razz

Razz is a game that is won by the lowest hand. The procedure and rules for Razz are basically the same as those used for Seven Card Stud.

The game should be limited to eight players.

The players are usually required to post an ante.

Starting to the left of the dealer, two rounds of cards are dealt facedown and one round is dealt faceup to each of the players.

After each player receives three cards, the first round of betting takes place.

The player with the highest upcard is required to make the opening bet.

An ace is used as a low card.

In the event two cards of the same rank are dealt, the cards are then ranked by suit. The highest ranking suit will start the first round of betting.

After the player with the highest card makes the opening bet, the following players may fold, call or raise the bet.

When the first round of betting is completed, the dealer will burn the top card of the deck and then deal another round of cards faceup to the remaining players in the hand.

The player with the lowest hand showing must bet or check. An open pair does not change the betting limit on fourth street.

If two or more hands are of equal ranking, the player closest to the left of the dealer must act first.

The dealer must burn the top card of the deck before dealing each round of cards.

The next two rounds of cards are dealt faceup.

A round of betting takes place after each round of cards is dealt.

The final round of cards is dealt facedown to each of the remaining players.

After all the bets are made in the final round, if more than one player remains, a showdown of the hands is required to determine the winner.

Each player must use five of his seven cards to make the best low hand. The best possible hand is A-2-3-4-5.

Straight and flushes do not count in establishing a hand. Only the numerical value of the cards is used to make the hand.

All seven cards must be exposed at the showdown.

The player with the lowest hand is declared the winner.

A player must have all seven cards to be eligible to win the pot. If the player does not have seven cards, his hand is declared a dead hand.

If a player picks up his upcards prior to calling the bet, his hand is declared dead. A player may pick up his cards after he calls the bet.

Before the final bet is made, the player may not rearrange his upcards.

CHAPTER

27

DRAW POKER

Draw Poker

Each player begins with five cards. He then has an opportunity to discard as many as five cards. His discards are then replaced by the dealer.

The high hand wins the pot.

A rotating button is used to denote the dealer position. The player immediately left of the dealer is dealt in first. This player also has the opportunity to discard and draw first.

The dealer must burn the top card of the deck before dealing the drawing round.

An exposed card before the draw must be kept by the player. An exposed card on the drawing round must be replaced at the completion of the drawing round by the top card of the deck. The player does not have the option of keeping the exposed card.

If there are not enough cards in the deck to complete the drawing round, the dealer must deal down to the last card. He then shuffles the burn card and the discards to complete the drawing round.

The last card of the deck is never used.

An ante is sometimes used and/or a small and big blind is put up by the first and second player immediately to the left of the button. The system and the amount are determined by house rule.

The number of raises allowed is also determined by house rule.

In the event of a tie hand, the pot is split. An odd chip is given to the player closest to the left of the dealer.

CHAPTER

28

TRIPLE DRAW DEUCE-TO-SEVEN

Triple Draw Deuce-To-Seven

The game is played using five cards to create the lowest hand.

A rotating dealer button is used.

A small blind and a big blind is placed by the two players immediately left of the dealer button.

The game should be played by a maximum of six players.

Each player is dealt five cards and then a betting round takes place.

A player is allowed to draw up to four cards per round.

The dealer must burn a card before each drawing round.

In triple draw there are three drawing rounds.

The best hand is 2-3-4-5-7. Aces are used as a high card only. Straights and flushes count as a high hand.

The betting is initiated by the player immediately left of the dealer button.

On the initial round of dealing, a ten or below exposed card must be kept by the player. A jack or higher must be replaced after all the cards are dealt by the top card of the deck. The exposed card is used as the burn card.

If two or more cards are exposed on the initial round, it is a misdeal.

On all subsequent dealing rounds, all exposed cards must be kept by the players.

In the event there are not enough cards to complete the drawing round, the cards will be dealt down to the last card and then the prior discards and the burn cards must be shuffled and dealt. The cards discarded for that round must not be used.

The last card of the deck can never be used.

House rules dictate the number of raises that are allowed. If only two players remain in the hand, unlimited raising is allowed.

CHAPTER

29

HIGH HAND JACKPOTS TEXAS HOLD'EM

High Hand Jackpots Texas Hold'em

High hand jackpots are becoming more popular than the Bad Beat Jackpots with both the players and the poker room management due to the following reasons:

1) The players hit frequency occurs more often.
2) The amount of the prize money is limited to $599, which negates tax obligations.
3) The hit frequency puts more playable money in the hands of the players. This will cause the player to remain in the game.
4) The lower per hit payout diminishes the desire to cheat in order to win the jackpot.

A high hand is defined as a hand, which matches one of the ranked hands, designated to win a share of the jackpot pool.

A recommended jackpot high hand schedule is made up of 26 possible high hands. This would start at four deuces and go all the way up to a royal flush in spades.

In order for a hand to be eligible for a high hand jackpot payout, both cards in the players hand must be used to make the high hand. Kickers are not considered part of the high hand.

When a player makes an eligible high hand, he will receive the amount then designated as the current amount available for that particular high hand.

In order to be eligible to win a high hand jackpot the following requirements must be satisfied:

1) The pot must contain at least $10 after the pot is raked for the jackpot pool.
2) The deck must be counted and verified to contain 52 cards. If the deck does not contain the proper number of cards, the jackpot payout is declared ineligible.
3) The high hand does not need to be played in a hand that goes all the way to the showdown. A player may collect the high hand payout even if their bet is not called.

4) It is possible for multiple high hand jackpots to hit in a single hand. In this event, each player receives the payout amount designated for that particular hand.

The daily jackpot drop will be distributed evenly between the 26 eligible hands using the following restrictions:

1) The high hand payout is limited to $599 per hand classification. When it reaches $599, that hand will not receive any more jackpot funds until it is hit.

2) When a high hand jackpot is hit, the amount of the payout for that hand will be reset to a predetermined starting amount.

When an eligible high hand is hit, the hand is announced by the dealer and verified by the Poker Room Shift Manager.

The funds will be paid in casino chips from the jackpot impress bank. This impress bank is refunded daily from the jackpot drop.

The winning player must sign all the required paperwork prior to receiving the jackpot payout.

No verbal collusion is allowed during the course of a jackpot hand.

CHAPTER

30

BAD BEAT JACKPOTS

Bad Beat Jackpots

A bad beat jackpot is one of the most popular marketing promotions that many cardrooms offer.

It has a great appeal to both the player and the cardroom management. It gives the player an opportunity to receive a large payout without a high risk. Poker room managers like it because it brings players to their games at no cost to them.

The bad beat jackpot is funded from a rake at the games from the player's money that is put in the pot. It is usually raked at 50c to $1.00 per hand.

Most bad beat jackpots are offered for a specific game. In other words, hold'em has its own jackpot as does each other game.

The jackpot amount will vary due to the different amounts of play each respective game receives.

Sometimes, management will make a decision to guarantee a minimum amount for the jackpot payoff and sometimes management will actually "**seed**" the jackpot with a set amount to get it started.

Because this is a marketing promotion offered by the various poker rooms, the qualifying requirements to win the jackpot do not reflect an industry standard. It varies by the decision of management or local gaming authority.

It is not uncommon for the qualifying requirements to change within a specific room several times within a 30 day period.

Naturally, the qualifying requirements must be posted in a conspicuous place for all of the players to read and when the qualifying requirements are changed, the players must be made aware of the changes before the jackpot hits. The changes and the date and time of the changes must be made public.

The following is a basic, general set of qualifying requirements that could be used to establish a bad beat jackpot:

1) Each game has its own jackpot.
2) The jackpot amount is posted in public view.
3) Four (4) or more players must be in the game at the time the jackpot is hit.
4) The losing hand must be four deuces or better.
5) Both holecards must be used by both the winning and losing hand.
6) The hand must go to the showdown.
7) The pot must be raked.

8) The jackpot rake contribution is made.

9) Players must play their hands independently.

10) Players are not allowed to reveal their hands until after the final betting round and then the showdown may commence.

11) The jackpot is paid as follows:
   a) 50% to the losing hand
   b) 25% to the winning hand
   c) 25% to the active players on the table

This payout structure is determined by each casino.

12) An active player is a player who participated in the hand at its beginning by being dealt into the hand.

Management Procedure
Bad Beat Jackpot

When the bad beat jackpot hits, a specific procedure must be followed by the poker room management to insure the integrity of the jackpot promotion.

This procedure varies according to the policy of each respective poker room manager/casino.

The following is a very general procedure that could be used in most poker rooms:

1) Dealer notifies the poker room shift manager.

2) Shift manager verifies the hands that qualify as the winning and losing hands.

3) Poker room shift manager notifies surveillance of the jackpot.

4) Poker room shift manager obtains I.D. from all of the players participating in the jackpot payoff.

5) Poker room shift manager and the dealer check the deck.

6) Poker room shift manager notifies the casino shift manager.

7) Poker room shift manager and the casino shift manager review the surveillance tape of the hand.

8) Poker room shift manager completes a bad beat jackpot report.

9) Casino shift manager double checks the bad beat jackpot report and signs it.

10) Poker shift manager and casino security present the bad beat jackpot report to the cage for payment.

11) Poker shift manager and security return to the poker room with the money to pay the players.

12) All required currency transaction reports must be completed and verified before payment can be made to the players.

13) If a player is unable to provide proper identification, the money due him will be deposited in the casino cage until the player furnishes his identification.

14) All original paperwork is deposited in the cage for transfer to the accounting department and copies are kept in the poker room.

Bad Beat Jackpot Report

Jackpot Amount $ _____

Bad Beat Winner $ _____50%

Winning Hand $ _____25%

Other Players $ _____25%

Bad Beat Hand   _____

Amount $ _____

Name_____

Winning Hand   _____

Amount $ _____

Name_____

Player Name_____ Player Name _____

Amount $_____ Amount $_____

Player Name_____ Player Name _____

Amount $_____ Amount $_____

Player Name_____ Player Name _____

Amount $_____ Amount $_____

Player Name_____ Player Name _____

Amount $_____ Amount $_____

Casino Shift Manager   Poker Room Shift Manager

_____ Dealer _____   _____ Cage Cashier _____

CHAPTER

31

TOURNAMENT PROCEDURES

Tournament Procedures

Tournaments have become one of the largest and most popular segments of poker since the inception of the *World Poker Tour.*

The television exposure that has resulted from the *World Poker Tour* and the televising of the *World Series of Poker* has created an incredible growth explosion in the number of people who play poker on the internet, in casinos, and at home.

Due to this explosion in the number of players, especially people who play in tournaments, many of the most influential poker industry leaders recognized the need to create a standard set of tournament rules.

This need brought about the creation of the *Tournament Director's Association* (TDA) by Linda Johnson, Jan Fisher, Matt Savage and David Lamb.

The TDA has done a great job of bringing a very high quality set of standard procedures that are used in most of today's tournaments.

The following is the Mission Statement of the TDA

Their website address is pokerTDA.com.

Poker Tournament Directors Association
TDA Mission Statement

To adopt basic standards, rules and procedures that will positively impact the Poker Industry by inviting tournament directors, players and media representatives to discuss, evaluate and review proposed rules.

The TDA is comprised of a group of poker room personnel from around the world objective is to draft a standardized set of rules of poker tournaments. They meet annually to discuss the addition of new rules and to amend or eliminate current rules. The TDA was founded by Matt Savage, David Lamb, Linda Johnson and Jan Fisher in 2001.

CHAPTER

32

POKER DIARIES

Poker Diaries

Another good marketing promotion for your poker room is to make a poker diary that the player will keep and use for a full year.

A diary should contain pertinent information about your poker room, such as; games offered, tournament schedules, bad beat jackpots and any other information you want the player to have relative to your room.

The diary should also contain forms that the player can use to record his travel, room, food and miscellaneous expenses relative to his poker activities.

It should also contain the names and dates of the major tournaments throughout the poker world.

Attached are two (2) simple forms that could be used to record the player's actual open poker game records and his tournament records.

Each poker record diary should have at least 12 pages of each record form. This would allow the player to use a different page for each calendar month.

How extensive you make the record diary book depends on you and how you plan to use it as a part of your room's marketing program.

On the following pages are examples:

Tournaments

Date	Casino	Game	Limit	Buy-In	#Players	Finish	W/L	Total

Tournaments_____Av. Buy-In_____Av. Finish_____

Total Buy-In _____Av. Win _____

Total W/L _____Av. Loss _____

Open Games

Date	Casino	Game	Limit	Buy-In	Win	Loss	Total

Sessions played_____   Total win/loss $_____   Av. Win Session $_____

Session Won_____   Av. Loss Session $_____

Session Lost_____   Av. Win_____Loss_____

CHAPTER

33

GLOSSARY

Glossary

There is no way to provide you with a complete glossary of terms; some of the most common terms are defined for you as follows:

Action- A fast game with lots of betting and raising; the betting, checking, calling or raising by a player.

All blue- A flush, generally in spades; also, all pink, all green, all red, and so on.

All in- Having put all of your chips in play into the pot.

All in bet- Betting the remainder of your chips.

Ammo, or ammunition- Chips or money available for play.

Ante- Money that each player is required to put into the pot before the cards is dealt, usually in a stud game.

Ante up- A common term used by the dealer when asking players to put their antes in front of them.

Baby- A small card, usually a deuce through a five.

Backdoor- Making a hand that you originally weren't trying to make by drawing more than one card.

Bad beat- Having a big hand beaten by someone making a long shot draw.

Bad beat story- The saga of a bad beat, usually told to anyone who will listen. Do not get into the habit of telling these stories; in reality, no one wants to hear them.

Bankroll, or BR- Money that is available for playing poker, and usually is kept separate from everyday funds, either physically or by bookkeeping methods.

Bar- To exclude someone from playing-that is, to bar a player.

Beat the board- In hold'em, having a hand that is better than the five community cards; cant beat the board is the opposite, and means playing the board.

Belly buster- An inside-straight draw, such as 4-5-7-8.

Bet- To wager or put money into the pot; to initiate the betting action.

Bet blind or bet dark- To wager without looking at your cards or before the cards are dealt.

Bet on the come- To wager on a hand that is yet to be completed; that is, a drawing hand wager.

Bet out or turn- Placing a wager before it is your turn to act.

Betting round- A complete wagering cycle in a hand of poker after all players have bet, called, folded or checked.

Big-bet poker- Any betting structure where the maximum wager is unlimited or controlled by the size of the pot, such as no-limit or half-pot limit.

Big slick- An Ace and a King.

Blank- A card that is of no value to your hand and seems to be of no value to your opponent.

Blind- A bet made before the cards are dealt in flop and draw games to open the betting.

Bluff- Betting a worthless hand knowing that the only way to win the pot is for no one to call you.

Board- The community cards in flop games and the upcards in stud games.

Boat- A full house, full boat; three of a kind and a pair.

Boxed card- A card, which appears face up in the center of the table.

Brick- A card that is "useless" to anyone.

Bullet – An ace.

Bump- A novice's term for raise; to increase the size of the previous bet, usually double the amount.

Burn card- The top card on the deck before each dealing round; this card is always buried facedown under the chips by the dealer before a round of cards is delivered to the players.

Button- The round disk placed in front of the player who receives the last card, acts last, and is theoretically the dealer in flop games; it moves clockwise one position after each hand.

Buy-in- The amount of chips or money required to enter a poker game.

Cage teller or cashier- Where players buy or cash in playing chips.

Call- To put chips into the pot that match the previous bet.

Called hand- A hand that has been bet and called and must be shown to win the pot.

Calling station- A player who plays unaggressively but calls most bets and therefore is difficult to bluff.

Cap- the number of raises allowed or the total dollar amount of all bets and raises allowed.

Card rack- A player who seemingly gets more than his fair share of good cards.

Cards speak- The ranking of a shown hand regardless of how it is verbally described.

Case card- The last remaining card of a particular rank or suit.

Chase- Playing with a worse hand than an opponent and trying to catch up and win.

Check- The same as pass; opting to remain in the hand but not bet, also used interchangeably with the term chip, as in gaming chip.

Check blind- The same as check dark, passing before seeing your card or cards.

Check raise- Passing and allowing another to bet, then raising that bet.

Chop the blinds- Also chopping; players agree to take back their posted blinds without playing out the hand if no one else calls or raises.

Cold call- Calling a bet or bets without previously having put money into the pot.

Color change- The same as color up; trading chip denominations either higher or lower.

Community card(s) – Card(s) used by everyone involved in the pot the boardcards in flop games and seventh street in a stud game when the dealer runs out of cards.

Concealed pair- In stud, when the first two downcards are of the same rank.

Connectors- Two sequential holecards in a hold'em hand.

Constant moving button- A button that is in front of an active player at all times.

Counterfeit- Having a card appear on the board that duplicates one in your hand, giving you a worse hand and generally costing you all or part of the pot.

Cover card- A plastic card used during the cut process and then to conceal the bottom card of the deck.

Cowboy- King.

Cracked- Beaten.

Dead hand- A hand that can't win or has been fouled for some reason.

Dead money- Money that is taken into the center of the pot and is not considered part of a particular player's bet.

Dealer button- The same as the button; position of the last player to act.

Decision- The determination made by the house to resolve a conflict in a game.

Deuce- Two.

Discard- Throw away a hand.

Discard pile- The muck; the pile of cards in front of the dealer where dead cards go and where all cards get reassembled before the start of the next hand.

Doorcard- The first upcard in stud.

Double belly buster- Also double gutshot; a straight draw in which hitting either one of two inside cards makes the hand.

Double nuts- The same as nut-nut; in a split-pot game, the best possible hand in each direction.

Downcard- Holecards in stud.

Draw- The exchanging of cards by a player, (after the initial round of betting), as in the game of draw poker.

Drawing hand- A poker hand that needs to be completed by drawing a card(s); the opposite of a pat hand.

Draw out- Overtaking a better hand by drawing a card to beat it.

Draw to- Drawing a card(s) to make a specific hand.

Duke- Big hand, usually the nuts.

Dummy up- Be quiet, the conversation is over.

Early position- The positions to the immediate left of the blinds or dealer; one of the first to act on each betting round.

Eight or better- The qualifier in a high-low split game; the low hand's biggest card may be only as high as an eight to be eligible to win the pot.

86- To bar or exclude; not allowed to patronize.

Exposed card- A faceup card in a stud game or a card that is inadvertently turned up by a player or dealer.

Facecard- A jack, queen, or king; also called a paint.

Family pot- A hand played by all of the players at the table.

Fast game- A game with lots of betting and raising, lots of action.

Fifth street- In stud, the fifth card to each player; in flop games, the last or river cards.

Filet- Slang for full house.

Fill up- To complete a hand by making a full house.

Filly- Slang for full house.

Fixed limit- Any betting structure where there is a betting limit on each player's bet.

Flash- To expose your holecards, either accidentally or on purpose.

Flexible limit- Any betting structure where there is a fixed upper limit but variable range on each betting round, such as, "one to four dollar limit".

Floorperson- A supervisor who, among other duties, handles disputes at the table.

Flop- In hold'em and Omaha games, the three cards simultaneously turned up in the center as community cards; the first three center upcards after the first round of betting.

Flop a set- To make three of a kind with the first three community cards.

Flush- Five suited cards; also, having lots of money.

Fold- To throw away your hand; having no further interest in the pot.

Forced bet- A mandatory bet to start the action; in stud, it's the low card by suit; in flop games, it's a blind.

Fouled hand- A dead hand; a hand that has come into contact with the muck and/ or discards, contains the wrong number of cards, contains a card that has been dropped on the floor, and so on. This hand is ineligible to win the pot and a floorperson has the discretion to call a hand dead.

Four-flush- Four suited cards.

Fourth street- In stud, the fourth card to each player; in flop games, the fourth or turn card, the first card after the flop.

Free card- A card that is received as a result of no bet by anyone on a particular round, giving those in the pot the next card without having to pay off a bet.

Freeroll- A hand, usually in flop games, in which players are tied and should split the pot, but one has a redraw to claim the entire pot.

Full boat- Full house.

George- Generous or very good.

Getting your hand cracked- Getting beaten, usually by a hand coming from behind and outdrawing you.

Give action- Gamble knowingly.

Grind it out- To play a low-limit, very solid game with not a lot of gamble.

Gutshot- Inside card to a straight.

Heads up- Two players in the pot or game.

Heart- Courage, fortitude.

Help a hand- To improve a holding on the draw.

Here to there- A straight, five cards in numerical sequence.

Hidden pair- Downcards containing two of the same rank.

Hidden trips- Downcards containing three of the same rank, or a concealed pair matching one of the upcards.

High- a game in which the highest hand wins the pot.

High-Low Split Eight or Better- A version of high-low poker in which a winning low hand must satisfy an eligibility requirement of a low hand in value of 8 or lower.

High-Low Split- A form of poker in which there is a winner for both the highest and lowest ranking hands.

Hit your kicker- To catch a card that is the same rank as your side or nonpaired cards.

Hogger- A pot that is scooped in high-low; the entire pot is won in a split game.

Holecards- Facedown cards.

Hook- Jack.

H.O.R.S.E. – A poker game that rotates five different games; hold'em, Omaha High-Low, Razz, Stud, and Stud High-Low Split Eight-or-Better.

Horse- One who's been staked to play.

Hot- Catching good cards and running well; also, angry or mad.

Human card rack- An individual who seems to run lucky; always catching better than average cards.

Idiot end (of straight) – In flop games, the low end of a possible straight on the board.

Immortal nuts- An unbearable hand in a given situation; a lock.

"I'll wait"- The same as "I'll check"; not wishing to make a bet.

Jack it up- Raise the pot.

Jackpot poker- A bad-beat giveaway in which a bonus is paid in some houses by a player-funded prize pool for extremely rare hand-over-hand situations.

Jam-up game- An action game, one with lots of betting and raising.

Jam-up person- A good guy.

Juice- Rake or vig(orish); the cost to play.

Keep you honest- Comment made when making a questionable call out of fear of being bluffed.

Kicker- Side card that is not paired; used to determine the winning hand.

Kicker trouble- Having the second-best side card and losing the pot.

Kill- In designated games an additional blind is posted by the scooper of the previous hand, or the winner of two hands in a row.

Kitchen poker- A small home game.

Knuckle it- Check the hand, no bet.

Lady- Queen.

Lammer- Button used to denote table activity.

Last to act- Button position or the player to the immediate right of the high hand.

Leak- Weakness in your game or other bad habit that costs money.

Leg up- In a kill game, when you must win two hands in a row to "kill it"; winning the first of the two is considered a leg up.

Limit poker- A game in which the minimum and maximum bet or raise a player can make is fixed.

Limp in- Call with a weak hand, or merely call when you could raise.

Lineup- The competition at your table.

List- The sign-up board for the game.

Live cards- Cards still available in the deck.

Live one- Loose, action player.

Lobby- Walk around away from the game, sits out awhile.

Lock- The nuts, an unbeatable hand in a given situation.

Lockup- A reserved seat for an incoming or moving player.

Loose- Opposite of tight, play lots of hands and call many bets.

Low- A game of poker in which the lowest hand wins the pot.

Main pot- Called action that an all-in player can win.

Make a play- Bluff at the pot, or raise, as the only way to win it.

Make up the binds-After the blind bets have passed, a player who missed the blinds posts blinds behind the button.

Marker- IOU.

Meet- Call the bet.

Minimum betting games- The smallest denomination of chip that is permitted to be wagered in the game once antes and blinds are posted.

Misdeal- An error occurring on the deal that requires the cards to be reshuffled and redealt.

Miss the flop- Holecards not connected to the flop in anyway.

Missed- Didn't make the hand that you w ere drawing to.

Monster- Huge, powerful hand.

Mortal nuts- Same as nuts; a lock, unbeatable hand.

Motion- Movement of the hand to indicate intention of action, motion may be binding.

Moves- Fancy plays, not always ethical.

Muck- Fold; also the discard pile.

Multiway- More than two players involved.

Needle- Pick on someone or someone's play; annoy verbally and personally.

Nickel- $5 chip, also called a redbird.

No-brainer- A hand that plays itself.

No limit poker- A player may wage any amount they have on the table on any round of betting.

No vacancy- A full house.

Nose open- A player on tilt; playing badly and punishing his chips.

Nut- Overhead or expenses, also the best hand.

Nut-nut- A lock on both high and low.

Offsuit- Unsuited cards.

On a rush- Catching lots of winning hands.

On board- Community cards in flop games, upcards in stud.

On the come- Drawing.

On the end- River or last card.

On the side- Not in the main pot, an additional pot created when a player has gone all in and the remaining players continue to bet.

On the turn- Fourth card.

On tilt- Out of control and playing wildly, usually cause by a bad beat or a series of loses.

Open-end straight- Four cards in sequence whereby drawing to either end completes a straight.

Open pair- In stud, a pair on board.

Opening bet- The first bet in a round of play.

Option- The big blind's chance to raise or check before the flop.

Out of turn- Incorrect nonsequential action.

Outs- Cards that can make your hand.

Overcards- Ones larger that cards that can be seen.

Paint- Facecard.

Pass- Check.

Pat hand- A hand that is played as dealt; no additional cards are needed.

Pay off- Call on the river with a probable losing hand.

Perfect-perfect- Drawing two cards in succession to make the best hand; same as runner-runner.

Pick up- Quit the game.

Piece of cheese- Bad hand.

Play back- Reraise.

Play behind- Playing while your chips are in transit after giving a chip runner cash for them.

Play the board- In hold'em, using all five community cards as your best playable hand.

Play tightly- To play conservatively.

Pocket- Downcards or holecards.

Pop it- Raise the pot.

Position- Where you are relative to the action.

Post- In hold'em, to put up (pay) a blind when entering a game, or make up blinds when they are missed by being away from the table.

Pot- The total amount anted and wagered by players during the game which is awarded to the winning player.

Pot limit poker- A player may bet or raise any amount up to the current size of the pot.

Powerhouse- Monster hand.

Premium hand- Top starting hand.

Proper action- Action that properly reflects the actual amount of the wager.

Proper card- The card a player would receive if there were no procedural irregularities on a deal.

Proposition player- A player who's paid to play with his own money, usually to help start games or to fill in when games are shorthanded.

Protect your cards- The player's responsibility to maintain control over his cards so that they will not become fouled.

Protected hand- A hand of cards which the player is physically holding or has placed one or more gaming chips upon.

Pumped up- Having lots of money.

Puppy feet- Club flush.

Quarter- $25 chip.

Rabbit hunting- Looking at, or asking to see, undealt cards to see what was coming and what hand you "would have" made.

Rack- A tray that holds 100 chips.

Rag- Weak hand or unrelated flop cards.

Rainbow- All different suits.

Raise- Increase the bet, must be at least double the amount of the original bet.

Raise on the come- Raise the pot with a drawing hand.

Rake- House vigorish, juice, table charge.

Rammer-jammer- A fast action player; one who plays lots of hands and bets and raises aggressively.

Random card- A card selected from a group of unknown cards, (cards that have not yet come into play), each having an equal chance of being chosen.

Random card concept- The idea that the substitution of a random card for a player's proper card, due to an irregularity, affords the player the same mathematical chances of winning the pot as before the irregularity occurred. It is assumed that the player has not been materially injured by that irregularity.

Rat-holer- One who discreetly takes chips or cash off the table before cashing out of the game, one who breaks table-stakes rules.

Read- Figure out the value of a hand that someone is holding.

Redbird- $5 chip.

Represent- To play a hand in a manner that leads opponents to believe that your hand is of a different value that it is.

River- The last card of the hand, fifth or seventh street.

Rock- A solid, tight, cautious player.

Rocket- Ace.

Rolled up- In a stud game, three of a kind (trips) to start.

Ruling- House decision to settle a dispute.

Runner-runner- Catching two cards in a row to make a hand.

Running pair- Two upcards that are a pair and were caught in succession.

Run over the game- Play fast and aggressively and win many pots as a result.

Rush- Making lots of winning hands in a row.

Sandbag- To slow-play a hand, usually with the intention of check-raising.

Scare card- An upcard in stud, or a boardcard in flop games, that most likely has helped someone's hand.

Scooper- In a split-pot game, a hand that wins both high and low.

Scramble- Mixing the cards facedown before the shuffle.

See- Call.

Set- Three of a kind; trips.

Setup- Two decks of make-up cards.

Seventh street- the last card; the river.

Shill- An employee who plays with house money for the sole purpose of helping to start or maintain games.

Shoot it up- Raise the pot.

Short buy-in- Less than the required amount to play in a particular game.

Shorthanded- A less than full game.

Shot taker- One who finds, and tries to exploit, a situation or angle.

Show one, show all- A cardroom rule stating that if a player shows his uncalled hand to another player in the game, he must, upon request, show it to the entire table.

Showdown- the end of the hand when cards are turned up and read by the dealer.

Side card- Kicker or unpaired card.

Side game- A ring game that is not a tournament event.

Side pot- A secondary pot that can't be won by an all-in player.

Sign up- To put your name on a list for a game.

Sixth street- In seven-card stud, the next to last card; in flop games, the turn card.

Slip it- To check it.

Slow-play- To underplay a big hand, hoping to trap many players.

Slow-roll- To knowingly have the best hand at the showdown and expose it only after the loser's hands are shown, leading another player to think that he has the winner.

Snapped off- To have a good hand beaten, usually by being outdrawn.

Soft break- The changing up of cash, usually for part cash and part chips; soft is cash and hard is chips.

Solid- A well-disciplined, good player.

Speeder- One who's playing fast; betting and raising aggressively.

Splash around- To become involved in many pots.

Splash the pot- To toss your chips directly into the pot, as opposed to setting them in front of you and near the pot.

Split pair- In a stud game, two cards of the same rank, one of which is an upcard and the other a holecard.

Split pot- A pot that is divided equally as a result of a tie hand between two players or a high hand and a low hand in a high-low split game.

Spread a game- To start a new game.

Spread limit- Variable betting within parameters as opposed to fixed limit; $1 to $5 vs. $3-$6.

Square up the table- To reposition players so that they are centered and spaced equally.

Stack- 20 chips.

Steal- Bluff.

Steal position- The button or the last position to act; because of this position, it has the best chance to steal the blinds or antes in an uncontested pot.

Steam- On tilt; out of control; reckless.

Stiff- Nontipper.

Straddle- An optional additional blind that is used to create action and promote more gambling in a game.

Steak- A run of cards, good or bad.

Street- Each round of dealt cards.

String bet- An illegal bet or raise; a bet made without verbal declaration and consisting of more than one forward motion or release of chips.

Structure- The antes, blinds, and betting limits that make up a particular game.

Structure limit- Predetermined betting amounts – for example, $5-$10.

Stub- The cards remaining after the deal has been completed.

Stuck- Losing.

Suck out- To outdraw a player who held a better hand.

Suited connectors- Two cards in sequence that are of the same suit.

Sweat- To take more than the needed time to squeeze out the last card to see if the hand has been made.

Sweater- One who watches a game, usually by sitting behind a player.

Table stakes- A universal public cardroom rule; only the chips and/or cash on the table before a hand begins can be used in the hand; all add-ons or buy-ins must be made between hands.

Tell- An unconscious or deliberate action or expression that reflects or misdirects the strength of a hand.

Third street- In stud, the doorcard or first upcard.

Throw the party- To lose lots of money, thus providing the "party" for the other players.

Ticket- Card.

Tight- Conservative.

Tilt- Out of control; playing wildly.

Toke- Tip (token of appreciation).

Trey- A three.

Trip up- To make a set (three of a kind).

Trips- Three of a kind; a set.

Turn card- In seven-card stud, fourth street; in flop games, the fourth upcard.

Under the gun- The first person to act.

Up to- The person whose turn it is to act.

Verbal declaration- Oral intention of action.

Vig(orish)- The rake, house drop.

Wait for the blinds- In flop games, to sit out until the blinds come around to you.

Wheel- The lowest straight, ace through five.

Wired- A pocket pair in stud on the deal.

World's fair- A big hand, usually the nuts.

CHAPTER

34

SUGGESTED READING

Suggested Reading

Super/System II
Doyle Brunson

Championship Hold'em
Tom McEvoy – T.J. Cloutier

More Hold'em Excellence
Lou Krieger

Hold'em Poker
David Sklansky

No Limit Texas Hold'em
Brad Daugherty – Tom McEvoy

Tournament Poker For Advanced Players
David Sklansky

Championship Stud
Dr. Max Stern – Linda Johnson – Tom McEvoy

The Psychology of Poker
Alan N. Schoonmaker, Ph.D.

The Professor The Banker and The Suicide King
Michael Craig

High-Low-Split Poker
Ray Zee

Casino Marketing
Nick Gullo

Texas Hold'em Study Guide
Nick Gullo

52 Tips For Texas Hold'em
Barry Shulman

Tournament Poker
Tom McEvoy

Winning Omaha/8 Poker
Lou Krieger – Mark Tenner

The Body Language of Poker
Mike Caro

Ace on the River
Barry Greenstein

Pizza Pasta and Poker
Vince Burgio

CHAPTER

35

TEXAS HOLD'EM STUDY GUIDE

TEXAS HOLD'EM
STUDY GUIDE
Beginning Players to Advanced Players

Texas Hold'em– A poker game using 5 of 7 cards to make the best possible high hand. Each player receives two cards in their hand and five community cards. He may use any combination of these seven cards to make his hand.

Hand Rankings

Straight flush, four of a kind, full house, flush, straight, three of a kind, two pair, one pair, high card

Suit Rankings

Spades, Hearts, Diamonds, Clubs

Starting Hand Information

Starting hands-169 possible starting hands.

Two card combinations–there are 1326 possible two card combinations

Pairs– there are six ways to make a specific pair

A-K– there are 16 ways to make an A-K combination

Any pair– You will average catching a pair every 17 hands

Aces– You will average catching a pair of aces every 221 hands The same for any specific pair

20 Good Starting Hands

AA	KK	QQ	JJ	TT
AKs	AQs	AJs	KQs	KJs
AK	99	QJs	JTs	AQ
KQ	ATs	KTs	QTs	88

(s) suited

Position is the most important aspect in determining your starting hand selection.

Early Position— You must be very selective in the starting hands you play from early position.

Blind Protection– It is not a wise play to automatically call a raise just because you are one of the blinds. Remember that you are in **E**arly position thereafter. A bet saved is often a bet earned.

Playing Your Hand

PAY ATTENTION—CONCENTRATE

Before the flop
What is my position
My starting hand
Who raised
What is the position of the raiser
After the flop (3 community cards)
What is the best hand on the flop
What is the best hand that can be made
Who bet and why
Who raised and why
Can I still draw a hand to win the pot
On the turn (4th community card)
What is the best hand on the turn
Who bet and why
Who raised and why
What is the best hand that can be made
What is the best hand that I can make
Will it win the pot
On the river (5th community card)
What is the best possible hand (nuts)
Who bet and why
Who raised and why
Do I have the winning hand
Can I make a winning play

Reading hands is <u>the</u> most important aspect of winning play. Try to read your opponents hand even when you are not in the hand.
TELLS-PAY ATTENTION– you will gain information about the play of your opponents by watching their actions and table demeanor.
Glance left before betting— you can gain information relative to the action the players following you are going to take.
FLOP-if the flop does not fit-**Fold.** Do not try to force a hand through. In the long run, it is a losing strategy.
Play your best– do not play when you are tired or have been drinking.
Best possible hand-you **MUST** always know the "nuts" at every level of the hand.

Kicker is a side card that is not paired but is used to determine the winning hand. It is the key to winning or losing many hands.
Suited cards are slightly more valuable than non-suited cards. Your cards should be played on the value of their rank, not only on the fact they are suited.
Most costly hands are the bottom ranked hand whether it is bottom pair, two-pair, trips, etc. Use caution when playing the bottom hand.
Best connectors is the J-10 because you can make a straight four ways and it will always be the "nuts".
Big pairs in early position may be raised to increase the size of the pot or to narrow the field of players.
Small pairs or small connectors may be played in late position against a large field and as cheaply as possible.
Limit hold'em is a game of big cards, patience and position.
Limit hold'em bluffing must be seldom used. In the long run, it is a losing strategy.
Ace anything should not be played in early position or if there is a raise in front of you. (anything = low card)

Pot odds is the size of the pot relative to the amount of money you are required to put in to call or to raise.

Implied odds is the projected size of the pot after all of the future bets are made relative to the amount of money you will be required to put into the pot.
Free card– if you raise on the flop, you will often receive a free card on the turn and the river.
Pre flop-respect the raise, especially from early position.

Outs– the number of cards that are still available in the deck that will make your hand.

Pair-if you are dealt a pair, you only have two cards (outs) to improve your hand.

Open ended straight after the flop has eight outs. You will make the straight 31.5% of the time. The odds of making it are 2.2 to 1 against you.

Flush– when you have two suited cards in your hand and flop two additional suited cards you have nine outs to complete the flush. You will make the flush 35% of the time. The odds are 1.9 to 1 against you.

You will **flop three of a kind** when holding a pair 11.8% of the time. The odds are 7.5 to 1 against you.

Pairing A-K- you will flop another A or K 32.4% of the time. The odds of pairing the A or K on the flop is 2.1 to 1 against you.

Nut straight-you must have the highest card of the straight in your hand or on the board.

Recommended Game Buy-in
Limit: Ten times the big blind
No Limit: Forty times the big blind

POKER DIARY– keep a record of your playing sessions. Note the date, casino, game, limits, time played and the win/loss of each session and month to date totals.

P. P. - Hold'em is a game of Patience and Position

Big Cards- Hold'em is a game of big cards, especially the kicker.

Cards Speak-the value of the hand is determined by the cards themselves, not by the verbal declaration of the players or the dealer.

Hand Protection- It is your responsibility to protect your hand.

Bankroll– Play at a level you can afford and feel comfortable playing.

POKER IS PEOPLE PLAYING PEOPLE USING CARDS

What are the odds of making my hand after the flop—How many outs do I have?

Outs	Favorable%	Odds Against
17	59.8%	.7 to 1
16	57.0%	.8 to 1
15	54.1%	.8 to 1
14	51.2%	1.0 to 1
13	48.1%	1.1 to 1
12	45.0%	1.2 to 1
11	41.7%	1.4 to 1
10	38.4%	1.6 to 1
9	35.0%	1.9 to 1
8	31.5%	2.2 to 1
7	27.8%	2.6 to 1
6	24.1%	3.1 to 1
5	20.3%	3.9 to 1
4	16.5%	5.1 to 1
3	12.5%	7.0 to 1
2	8.4%	10.9 to 1
1	4.3%	22.3 to 1

Simple Probability Formula

After the flop-Multiply the number of outs by four. Eight outs x 4 = 32% of making your hand.
After the turn-Multiply the number of outs by two. Eight outs x 2 = 16% chance of making your hand.
This formula is not 100% accurate but it will get you close enough under pressure.

Poker Etiquette
Do not ask to see the losing hand without having a specific reason for doing so.
Do not splash the pot with your chips.
Do not criticize another persons play.

Big Pairs-Raise to narrow the number of players against you. They go down in value against a large field.

A-K-Call, it is a drawing hand. If it hits, bet. If it does not hit or fit the flop, you can fold. The call also disguises the strength of your hand. (Nick's theory)

Game Type Analysis
Loose game-several players entering or raising the pot pre-flop on a continual basis with weak or marginal hands.
Tight game– a limited number of players entering or raising the pot pre-flop with good or premium hands.
Passive play—very little raising. Most of the action is a bet and a call. Most of the players are calling stations.
Aggressive play—a lot of raises and re-raises on each round by a limited number of players with good or premium hands.

Playing Strategy
Loose Game– opponents will play weaker hands and to the showdown. Play big cards. Avoid fancy plays. Do not bluff. Play more hands.
Tight Game– solid, aggressive play wins. Have patience. Position is important. Use the semi-bluff and bluff more often.
Big/Little Hands—A-6, K-3, Q-4, etc. Avoid playing them unless you are heads up. They are financial suicide.
Slow Play– Avoid in loose games. Use occasionally in limit games only when you have the "nuts" and your bet would cause the others to fold.
Short Handed– play aggressively with big cards. Use the semi-bluff more often.
Deceptive play– vary your style of play so that you are not an easy read for your opponents.

Winning players in the long run are tight and aggressive players.
Losing players are loose players and/or passive players. Calling stations cannot be winning players.

When Losing-play solid, tighter poker. Do not play looser to try to recover. Avoid going on tilt.

Tilt—every player suffers a bad beat or throws away the winning hand occasionally. It is a part of poker. A player on tilt is a losing player.

Created and written by:
Nick Gullo

Copyright—2004-2006
ISBN 0-9779301-1-4

Printed in the United States
By Bookmasters